BRIAN O'LEARY

POOLBEG

Galway County Libraries

1629
283

Hist 937
€10

Published 2005
by Poolbeg Press Ltd
123 Grange Hill, Baldoyle
Dublin 13, Ireland
E-mail: poolbeg@poolbeg.com

Typesetting, layout, design © Poolbeg Press Ltd.

1 3 5 7 9 10 8 6 4 2

A catalogue record for this book is available from the British Library.

ISBN 1-84223-240-1

Printed by
Betaprint, Ireland

www.poolbeg.com

Acknowledgements

Many thanks to my parents, Jim and Detta O'Leary, their combined fifty years'
experience as driving instructors proved an invaluable fountain of knowledge
during the preparation of this book.
Thanks to Brenda for her help and support.
Thanks to James Brady and Alan Pollock who gave generously of their time.
Thanks to Declan Hayes of the Department of Transport and
Peter Murphy of the National Safety Council for their wonderful help and advice.
Special thanks are due to Eamon Kennedy of the Department of Transport Driver
Testing Section for permission to use the driving test report card in this publication.

Get It!

CONTENTS

INTRODUCTION

Anybody can pass the driving test in a car. Good practice and knowing exactly what the tester requires of you is all it takes. This book examines the new tester's scorecard, with each individual heading and subheading taken apart in detail.

Whether it's your neighbour, your uncle, or someone in the pub, everyone seems to have a theory or opinion on how you'll pass or fail your test, but you can take these with a pinch of salt more often than not. This book is where the hard facts are, where you'll get straight answers about what you should and shouldn't do in every aspect of your driving test. It's an essential guide, put together by people with the experience to **know** what's needed to pass the test.

Don't worry – you won't find hundreds of pages of heavy reading inside! The written facts are kept to the essential minimum, while easy-to-understand, full-colour graphics are frequently used to illustrate points.

This book will **not** teach you how to drive from scratch. What it **will** do is show you exactly what's required to pass your driving test in a car. The sections contained will follow precisely the layout of the only document that matters on the day: the tester's scorecard, or 'Driving Test Report'. **This is a new scorecard, recently introduced, and therefore has not been dealt with by any previous book.**

If you've previously failed your test, you should find this book of particular help. The tester will have given you a marked report, but as they are not obliged to explain to you why you failed, you may be none the wiser as to the reasons, and unable to make head or tail of the various "**X**"s. With this book, you can now look up what was marked on the report, and see exactly what you did wrong. More importantly, you can see exactly what you need to do to avoid making the same mistakes again.

Remember, as said above, this is not a "learn-to-drive" book – we recommend you do that with a qualified driving instructor. But once you have learned to drive correctly, it'll help to "seal the deal". After you have passed your test, this book will remain a constant and reliable source of good driving advice. The full driving licence is a wonderful asset for anybody to have, so go out and **GET IT!**

How to use this book!

The sections in this book follow exactly the same layout and headings as the driving test 'Report' which the tester fills out during your test. If you have recently failed your test, you will have been given one of these reports. To examine how or why you failed, cross-check the sections marked on your sheet against the relevant section of this book. The book will clarify the main reasons for failure under each particular heading. More importantly still, it tells you how to avoid making these mistakes again.

This may be your first test. **How often do you get to see the exam paper before you sit an exam?** This book not only shows you the exam paper, but takes it apart and analyses it piece by piece. Even if you are an accomplished driver, you will probably admit to having **bad habits**. Assuming that you can already drive, we have the luxury of being able to concentrate on exactly what you need to do to pass your test.

We take each manoeuvre and deal with it under each specific heading. This means for example that in the section on 'Reverse: Observation', we deal only with the observation part of the reverse. If you are worried about how the tester would like to see you steer or use the clutch on the reverse, this is dealt with in the section 'Reverse: Competently.' The exact nature of each section means that the book is simple to follow and gives you the best possible idea of the standard by which the tester will rate your driving.

"Sometimes a picture can be worth a thousand words." Full colour and clear diagrams are used to great effect in this book. Studying a straightforward diagram can often be much more beneficial and enlightening than reading long passages of writing. The idea of this book is to use diagrams when necessary and wherever possible.

This book is not an interpretation of the law.

Copy of Driving Test Report

Applicant: _____ Date: _____ Reg No.: _____

FAULTS	Grade 1	Grade 2	Grade 3	FAULTS	Grade 1	Grade 2	Grade 3
1. RULES/CHECKS				**11. PROGRESS**	Maintain reasonable progress and		
2. POSITION	Position vehicle correctly and in good time				avoid undue hesitancy when		
On the Straight				Moving Off			
On Bends				On the Straight			
In Traffic Lanes				Overtaking			
At Cross Junctions				At Cross Junctions			
At Roundabouts				At Roundabouts			
Turning Right				Turning Right			
Turning Left				Turning Left			
Stopping				Changing Lanes			
Following Traffic				At Traffic Lights			
3. OBSERVATION	Take proper observation			**12. VEHICLE CONTROLS**	Make proper use of		
Moving Off				Accelerator			
Overtaking				Clutch			
Changing Lane				Gears			
At Cross Junctions				Footbrake			
At Roundabouts				Handbrake			
Turning Right				Steering			
Turning Left				Secondary Controls			
4. REACT TO HAZARDS	React promptly and properly to hazards			Technical Checks			
Reaction				Coupling/Uncoupling			
5. MIRRORS	Use properly, in good time and before signalling			**13. SPEED**	Adjust speed to suit/on approach		
Moving Off				Road Conditions			
On the straight				Traffic Conditions			
Overtaking				Roundabouts			
Changing Lanes				Cross Junctions			
At Roundabouts				Turning Right			
Turning Right				Turning Left			
Turning Left				Traffic Controls			
Slowing/Stopping				Speed Limit			
6. CLEARANCE/OVERTAKE	Allow sufficient clearance to			**14. TRAFFIC CONTROLS**	Comply with		
Pedestrians				Traffic Lights			
Cyclists				Traffic Signs			
Stationery Vehicles				Road Markings			
Other Traffic				Pedestrian Crossing			
Other Objects				Garda/School Warden			
Overtake Safely				Bus Lanes			
7. SIGNALS	Give correct signal in good time			Cycle Lanes			
Moving Off				**15. RIGHT OF WAY**	Yield right of way as required		
Overtaking				Moving Off			
Changing Lane				Overtaking			
At Roundabouts				Changing Lanes			
Turning Right				At Junctions			
Turning Left				At Roundabouts			
Stopping				Turning Right			
Cancel Promptly				Turning Left			
Hand Signals				**16. REVERSE**			
Beckoning Others				Competently			
Misleading				Observation			
8. MOTORCYCLES				Right of Way			
Safety Glance				**17. TURNABOUT**			
U-Turn: Control/Obs.				Competently			
Slow Ride				Observation			
Park On/Off Stand				Right of Way			
Walk Alongside				**18. PARKING**	Loading/Unloading/Passenger stops		
				Competently			
9. COURTESY				Observation			
10. ALIGHTING				Legally			

Department of Transport
An Roinn Iompair

DRIVING TEST REPORT

No. **415402**

Passed your Driving Test

Having passed your driving test you should nevertheless continue to pay particular attention to the faults marked overleaf without neglecting other aspects of your driving.

Failure of your Driving Test

Failure of the test arises where you incur any of the following:-
1 or more **grade 3** faults,
4 of the same **grade 2** faults for a single aspect,
6 or more **grade 2** faults under the same heading, or a total of
9 or more **grade 2** faults overall.
Up to a maximum of 4 **grade 2** faults may be recorded for any single aspect.

Grading of faults

Faults are graded as follows:-

Grade 1 (Green Area) Minor Fault, **Grade 2** (Blue Area) More Serious Fault, **Grade 3** (Pink Area) Dangerous/Potentially Dangerous or total disregard of traffic controls.

Grade 1 faults do not affect the test result.

A combination of 3 or more unanswered or incorrectly answered questions on the Rules of the Road/Checks, constitutes a **grade 2** fault. (Checks include doors closed safely, the headrest, mirrors, seat and seat-belt adjustment, and for motorcyclists, the helmet, gloves, boots and protective clothing).

3 or more hand signals not demonstrated correctly constitutes a **grade 2** fault.

3 or more Secondary Controls not demonstrated correctly constitutes a **grade 2** fault. (Secondary controls include temperature controls, fan, air vents, rear-window heater, wipers, windscreen washer, light switches, air intake control, rear fog light and air conditioner, if fitted).

Not operating a Secondary Control as required during the practical test can also constitute a fault.

Technical checks - all categories

Inability to describe a check on 3 or more of the following constitutes a **grade 2** fault:-

The tyres, lights, reflectors, indicators, engine oil, coolant, windscreen washer fluid, steering, brakes and horn. Where necessary, the bonnet should be opened and closed safely. For motorcyclists the checks can also include the chain, and the emergency stop-switch, if fitted.

For catergories C1, C, D1, D, EC1, EC, ED1 and ED technical checks include the following as appropriate to the category:-

The power assisted braking and steering systems, the condition of the wheels, wheel nuts, mudguard, windscreen, windows, wipers, air-pressure, air tanks, suspension, engine oil, coolant, windscreen washer fluid, the loading mechanism if fitted, the body, sheets, cargo doors, cabin locking, way of loading and securing the load, and checking and using the instrument panel and tachograph.

For catergories D1, D, ED1 and ED technical checks include controlling the body, service doors, emergency exits, first aid equipment, fire extinguishers and other safety equipment.

Coupling/Uncoupling includes:-

(a) Checking the coupling mechanism and the brake and electrical connections,

(b) Uncoupling and recouping the trailer from/to its towing vehicle using the correct sequence. The towing vehicle must be parked alongside the trailer as part of the exercise.

Parking in relation to categories EB, C1, C, EC1, and EC includes parking safely at a ramp or platform for loading/unloading.

Parking in relation to D1, D, ED1 and ED includes parking safely to let passengers on or off the bus.

Motorcyclists

Safety glance means looking around to check blind spots as necessary

Preparing for your next Driving Test

In preparing for your next test you should pay particular attention to the items which have been marked. Further information on these and other aspects of the test are contained in the booklet entitled "The Rules of the Road" which is available at book shops and in the leaflet "Preparing for your Driving Test" which is issued with the acknowledgement of your application.

Note

Items on which faults occurred during your driving test are marked overleaf. The driver tester is not permitted to discuss the details of the test.

RULES OF THE ROAD/CHECKS

On entering the test centre, the first thing the tester will do is check your provisional licence. This is to confirm your identity and also to see that the licence is both current and valid for the category of vehicle you will be driving. The tester will then ask you to sign a form stating that the vehicle you are providing for the test is in roadworthy condition, and that you are insured to drive it during the course of the test. You will then be asked a number of oral questions on the Rules of the Road and asked to identify some Road Signs. It is very important to do some revision on the Rules of the Road prior to the test, even though you may have already passed a theory test. Under the latest marking system, failure to answer correctly three or more questions or signs would constitute a Grade 2 fault. Start as you mean to go on - confident, concise and accurate answers will impress the examiner before you ever sit into the car. Here is a list of the most commonly asked questions.

 Q. *You are approaching a set of Traffic Lights and the Amber light is showing. What would you do?*

A. Stop if it is safe to do so.

 Q. *What colour comes after Amber?*

A. Red.

 Q. *You are approaching a set of Pedestrian Lights and the lights are flashing Amber, what would you do?*

A. You may proceed with caution provided it is safe to do so.

 Q. *What do Double Yellow Lines mean?*

A. No parking at any time.

 Q. *What do Continuous White Lines on the road mean?*

A. Keep left and do not cross the line except in case of emergency or for access.

Q. *What does a Broken Yellow Line along the edge of a major road mean?*
A. It marks off the edge of the road and shows where the hard shoulder begins.

 Q. *What is the rule at the Yellow Box Junction?*
A. Do not enter the box unless your exit ahead is clear. However you may enter the box and wait if you are turning right, so long as you don't block traffic with right of way. *(see page 34)*

 Q. *What do Zigzag markings either side of a Zebra Crossing mean?*
A. Do not park in that area and do not overtake on the approach to the crossing.

 Q. *When is it possible to Overtake on the Left?*
A. If the vehicle in front is turning right and you are going either straight on or turning left. Also in lanes of traffic where the traffic in the right-hand lane is going more slowly than the traffic in the left-hand lane.

 Q. *What road users and vehicles are not allowed to use Motorways?*
A. Learner Drivers. Cyclists. Pedestrians. Animals. Invalid carriages. Vehicles under 50cc. Slow vehicles under 50km/h.

 Q. *At a Roundabout, what traffic should you give right of way to?*
A. Give way to traffic coming from the right and any traffic already on the roundabout.

 Q. *At a Junction with roads of equal importance which traffic would you give right of way to?*
A. Traffic coming from the right and any traffic already crossing at the junction as you are on the approach.

 Q. *What does a Broken White Line in the centre of the road mean?*
A. You may cross if it is safe to do so.

Q. *If there are Double White Lines in the middle of the road, and the line nearest to you is continuous, what does this mean?*
A. The driver must obey the line nearest to them. In this case do not cross on the continuous line.

Q. *What does a Single Yellow Line along a kerb mean?*
A. No parking during business hours.

 Q. *When would you use Dipped Headlights?*
A. When meeting traffic while driving at night. When following behind traffic that you do not intend to overtake. In lit up areas. During bad weather ie. heavy snow, rain or fog. At dawn and dusk.

 Q. *When may you use the Right-hand Lane of a Dual-carriageway?*
A. You may drive in the right-hand lane when overtaking or when you intend to turn right a short distance ahead.

 Q. *Are you allowed to drive on the Hard Shoulder?*
A. The hard shoulder is not an extra traffic lane and should normally be used only by pedestrians and cyclists. Traffic may temporarily use the hard shoulder to allow faster vehicles to pass provided there are no pedestrians or cyclists using it.

 Q. *What are the main differences between Motorways and Ordinary Roads?*
A. The speed limit on a motorway goes up to 120km/h. It is normally prohibited to stop or park on any part of the motorway. You must not make 'U' turns. Motorways do not have right-hand turns, junctions or roundabouts and must be joined and exited using a slip road tothe left.

 Q. *What is the National Speed Limit for a car on a national primary road?*
A. 100km/h.

 Q. *What is the normal stopping distance for a car traveling at 50km/h on a dry road/ wet road?*
A. Approx. 24 metres dry road/ 31 metres wet road.

 Q. *What is the normal stopping distance for a car traveling at 100km/h on a dry road/ wet road??*
A. Approx. 75 metres dry road/ 130 metres wet road. .

Learn all road signs! This oral part of the test will not be as detailed as the new Theory test but you will need to know all signs. **Study the illustrations on page 9.**

After the road sign questions, the tester will say, 'That is the end of the oral part of your test. We will now go out to your car for the practical part.' You will then lead the tester out to your car. It is at this point that he will get you to show that your brake lights and indicator lights are in working order. The tester will also check that

Galway County Libraries

your tax, insurance and NCT discs are valid and displayed properly. He will also have a look to see that your tyres are not visually defective i.e. of less than 1.6mm thread depth.

You will now be asked to show your knowledge of some basic technical checks on your vehicle. Following this, he/she will get you to run through some of the secondary controls. The new 'Technical checks' element of the test and the 'Secondary controls' element are dealt with in more detail on page 29 as they are marked under the heading of 'Vehicle Controls'.
Before you are ready to move off, you must ensure that all doors are securely closed, your seat belt is fastened and the gear lever is in neutral before you start your engine. These are the 'Checks' referred to at the heading of this chapter.

Your Notes:

REGULATORY SIGNS

NEW METRIC
SPEED LIMITS

STOP SIGN   NO RIGHT TURN   NO ENTRY   WEIGHT RESTRICTION   KEEP LEFT

NO PARKING   PARKING PERMITTED   YIELD RIGHT OF WAY   GÉILL SLÍ   PASS EITHER SIDE

SCHOOL WARDENS SIGN   TAXI RANK   NO LEFT TURN   TURN LEFT   TURN RIGHT

CLEARWAY
STOPPING OR PARKING
PROHIBITED DURING
TIMES SHOWN

PEDESTRIAN ZONE
STREET TRAFFIC
PROHIBITED

CONTRA FLOW
BUS LANE

BUS LANE
(MAY ALSO BE
USED BY
TAXIS AND
CYCLISTS)

STRAIGHT
AHEAD ONLY

WARNING SIGNS

JUNCTION AHEAD WITH ROAD OR ROADS OF EQUAL IMPORTANCE

JUNCTION AHEAD WITH ROAD OF LESS IMPORTANCE

JUNCTION AHEAD WITH A MAJOR ROAD OR DUAL CARRIAGEWAY MARKED
BY A 'STOP' SIGN OR 'YIELD' RIGHT OF WAY SIGN

| DANGEROUS CORNER AHEAD | DANGEROUS BEND AHEAD | SERIES OF DANGEROUS CORNERS AHEAD | SERIES OF DANGEROUS BENDS AHEAD |

| ROAD NARROWS DANGEROUSLY AHEAD | HUMP BACK BRIDGE | SHARP DEPRESSION AHEAD | SERIES OF BUMPS OR HOLLOWS AHEAD |

WARNING SIGNS

POSSIBLE PRESENCE
OF RIDERS ON
HORSEBACK AHEAD

WARNING FOR SCHOOLS AND CHILDREN

TWO WAY
TRAFFIC

UNPROTECTED
CANAL OR
RIVER AHEAD

STEEP ASCENT
AHEAD

STEEP DESCENT
AHEAD

ROADWORKS
AHEAD

LEVEL CROSSING
AHEAD GUARDED
BY GATES OR
LIFTING BARRIERS

LEVEL CROSSING
AHEAD WITH
LIGHTS AND
BARRIERS

ROUNDABOUT
AHEAD

RESTRICTED
HEADROOM

SLIPPERY ROAD
AHEAD

TRAFFIC SIGNALS
AHEAD

LEVEL CROSSING
UNGUARDED BY
GATES OR LIFTING
BARRIERS

TUNNEL
AHEAD

OVERHEAD
ELECTRIC
CABLES

TRAMWAY
CROSSING
AHEAD

ROADWORKS SIGNS

ROADWORKS
AHEAD

TRAFFIC LIGHTS
AHEAD

CROSSOVER
TO RIGHT

ROAD NARROWS
FROM LEFT

DIVERTED TRAFFIC

DIVERTED TRAFFIC

MAJOR ROADWORKS
AHEAD

DETOUR

INFORMATION SIGNS

MOTORWAY SIGNS

END OF
MOTORWAY
500M

END OF
MOTORWAY

MOTORWAY AHEAD SIGN

MOTORWAY AHEAD SIGN

Positioning

POSITION VEHICLE CORRECTLY AND IN GOOD TIME

Fig. 01

ROAD POSITIONING ON THE STRAIGHT

The positioning of your car on the road is one of the most important aspects of driving. It is also one of the most common contributing factors for failure in the Irish driving test. Your position will be judged on the straight, on bends, making right and left turns, on one-way streets, at roundabouts and when overtaking. Throughout the test, you should position your vehicle correctly and in good time before attempting any manoeuvre. The examiner sees this as an essential sign of your regard for the safety and convenience of other road-users.

Examine the diagrams provided.

● POSITION ON THE STRAIGHT

A common mistake is driving too closely to or over the white line in the centre of the road. In general, keep well to the left during normal driving. Make sure that you do not drive too closely to parked vehicles or into drains at the roadside.
Stay approximately the width of a car door out from parked cars or drains.
On a one-way system you must stay in the left-hand lane unless directed otherwise.

● ON BENDS

One must be careful not to stay too tight to the corner on bends. Do not take the 'racing line' when rounding a corner. On narrow roads, move out slightly to a position which will allow oncoming traffic and pedestrians an early view of your approach. This is called the 'advantage position' and will enable you to react early should you meet a hazard. This is particularly true where there is no footpath or cycle lane. Do, however, keep inside the white line in the centre of the road unless you check your way is clear and signal to move out past something.

● IN TRAFFIC LANES

Keep within road lane markings. Only cross a lane marking if you have checked your mirrors and signalled to do so. In the absence of such markings you must mentally envisage where they should be. Always yield right of way to traffic in another lane.

● AT CROSS JUNCTIONS
Examine the diagram provided.

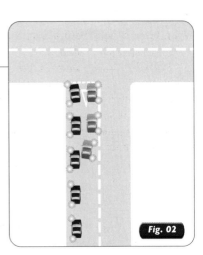
Fig. 02

● AT ROUNDABOUTS
Examine the diagrams provided.

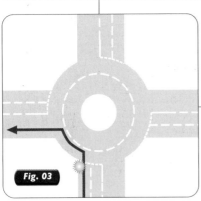
Fig. 03

TAKING THE FIRST EXIT

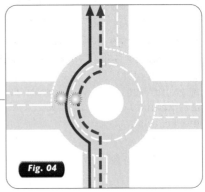
Fig. 04

**TAKING THE SECOND EXIT
(STRAIGHT AHEAD)**

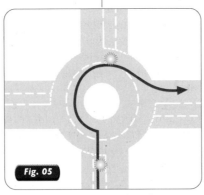
Fig. 05

TAKING THE THIRD EXIT

● Turning Right

When turning right from a main road onto a side road, mirror, signal, manoeuvre and move towards the white line in the centre of the road. Look into the roadway you intend to turn into and move into a position where the nose of your car is parallel with the white line in the centre of the sideroad. Begin to turn your wheel at this point so you make the turn as much at a right angle (90 degrees) as possible. On a one-way street assume that you have a left-hand lane and a right-hand lane and move over into the right-hand lane before making the turn. If the road you are turning into is also a one-way street, go around in the right-hand lane and gradually make your way back over towards the left. This is standard procedure on a one-way system. *Examine the diagram provided.*

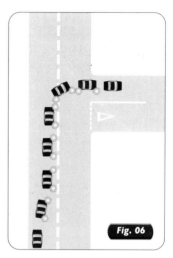

Fig. 06

TURNING RIGHT

● **Turning Left:** After checking your mirrors and indicating left, adjust your speed and begin your descent through the gears, keeping your speed under control. Keep your position towards the left and make your turning neatly, keeping well into the left. The most common positioning fault when turning left is swinging too wide and crossing the white line in the centre of the other road. On the other hand, it is also a common fault to cut the corner and clip the footpath with the back wheel. *Examine the diagram provided.*

● **Stopping:** When you are stopping in traffic, do not stop on the black and white stripes of a zebra crossing or on a yellow box junction when you are going straight ahead. When stopping at a junction, be careful not to stop too far out onto the road so as to cause an obstruction.

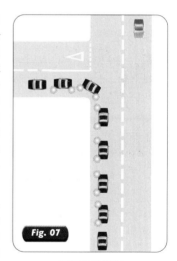

Fig. 07

TURNING LEFT

● **Following Traffic:** You must be able to stop your car within the distance in front of you that you see to be clear. Put simply, the faster you are travelling, the greater distance you should leave between yourself and the vehicle in front. On the open road, watch the car in front pass a stationary object, then repeat to yourself, "Only a fool breaks the two-second rule." If your own car has passed the object before you have finished this sentence, then you are too close! In very slow-moving traffic, make sure you can at least fully see the two back tyres under the car in front.

OBSERVATION

▶ *Take proper observation.*

● **Without a doubt, this is the most common area of failure in the test.**
To observe means to watch, to scrutinise and to pay attention to. Good drivers will be constantly alert and aware of other traffic and pedestrians in their surroundings. The following is a list of what appears on the examiner's scorecard under the heading of observation. Alongside each section are hints on how to correctly avoid being faulted. You will also be judged on your observation under the headings of Reverse, Turnabout and Parking and these will be dealt with in due course. In preparation for your test, it's a good idea to clear your windows of all unnecessary junk such as soft toys, large stickers and furry dice. You may not be taken out on your test if your side windows are blacked out (over-tinted, D.I.Y. style). Make sure your 'L' plates are placed in a position where they cause least obstruction to your view.

Fig. 08

● **Moving Off:** Before moving off, look in your inside centre mirror and outside right mirror. Turn your head to look over your right shoulder before pulling off. Looking over your shoulder will allow you to see into any blind spots. You will also be able to see any vehicles coming at you from junctions across the way, as well as anything small such as cyclists passing your shoulder. Make sure to look back in the direction you are travelling as you move off.

BLIND SPOTS

● **Overtaking:** Stay well back from the vehicle in front so your view is not restricted. Make sure there is no continuous white line in the centre of the road. Check your inside centre mirror and outside right mirror. Indicate right. Have a quick glance over your right shoulder before pulling off. Make sure you can see the vehicle you have just overtaken in your rear view mirror before indicating left and pulling back in.

● **Changing Lanes:** Before moving right, check your centre mirror then your outside right mirror before having a quick glance over your right shoulder. Before moving into a lane on your left, look in your inside mirror and your outside left mirror before having a quick look over your left shoulder, then moving to the left.

● **At Cross Junctions:** Check mirrors and signal to the appropriate side on approach. Coming in slowly, use the approach to begin looking in all directions. Don't wait until you stop or yield to begin looking. When you come into a junction with a yield sign, expect to have to stop. At the junction, lean well forward and look **both** ways regardless of which direction you are taking. If the junction is quite blind or if there is an obstruction to your line of sight (eg. a car parked on double yellow lines) creep out to the point where you can see. You must be able to see clearly both sides before moving off. Where one side is blinder than the other, look to the blindest side last. At the point where you begin to move, make sure you are looking in the direction you are going. **There may be a vehicle passing directly in front of you.** When you have moved off into the correct position, check your rear-view mirror.

● **At Roundabouts:** (If you need to change lanes on approach, follow the instructions provided above.) Begin to look both ways on approach, paying particular attention to traffic approaching from the right-hand side. When you see a clear gap in the traffic coming from your right, look left again to check traffic has not stopped before moving off. Having passed the exit before the one you intend to take, check your inside centre mirror and your outside left mirror, signal and look over your left shoulder before exiting.

● **Turning Right:** When turning right off a road, look in your inside centre mirror and your outside right mirror, signal right and move into position. When in position, look up the road to make sure your way is clear. **It is vital that you have a good look into the roadway you intend to turn into before you leave your position.** This last point is often neglected and therefore is a common fault.

● **Turning Left:** Check your inside mirror, your outside left mirror and signal, all in good time. Make sure to lean forward and have a good look into the sideroad before you commit yourself to the turn.

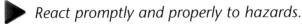

REACTION TO HAZARDS

▶ *React promptly and properly to hazards.*

The less actual driving experience you have, the greater risk there is of being faulted under this heading. **Anticipation** is the word a driving instructor will use to describe how to **avoid having to react suddenly** to a hazard. Whereas observation involves seeing what is actually happening, anticipation means predicting or thinking ahead to what **will** happen. The best way to improve your anticipation is by getting as much driving experience as possible in all road, weather and traffic conditions. You must prompt yourself to be constantly ready to "expect the unexpected". This is particularly important for test candidates who do not have the luxury of a lot of preparation time. Keep in mind that situations can change quickly from what you can observe to what might develop. Here are a few prime examples of anticipation in practice.

● **If you have right of way, never take for granted that you are going to get it.** Always do plenty of looking and be prepared to stop at a junction even when you have a green light. Remember! Green only means proceed if it is clear.

● **Beware if the car in front is crawling slowly.** The driver may be looking for a parking space or could be lost and looking for directions. The driver may suddenly stop or turn right or left without indication. Stay well back until you work out what the driver is doing. If the car stops beyond a vacant space, the driver may be about to reverse in. If you are too close you may have to reverse yourself.

● **Don't just look at the road or car directly ahead of you!** In traffic you must keep an eye on several cars ahead of you. When the brake lights of cars two or three spaces ahead of you come on, begin to decelerate and prepare to brake yourself. Going through a built-up area, you must pay attention to what is happening on footpaths and cyclepaths around you. Watch for pedestrians and cyclists who are so close that a sudden movement on their behalf would affect you. Children and the elderly deserve special attention. Children can lack road-sense while the elderly might be hard of hearing or slow on their feet.

● **Remember that the person in front might be a learner or bad driver.** When moving in slow-moving traffic, never go so close that you cannot see the rear tyres under the car in front. This rule of thumb should help you in case of sudden braking. At a junction on a slope, never stop too close to the car in front, as it may roll back.

● **Watch out during a shower of rain!** Pedestrians may run with their heads down or have umbrellas or hoods obscuring their view. The desire to seek shelter can often come at the expense of common sense. Pedestrians and cyclists often take greater risks during rain in the hope of getting to their intended destination more quickly.

MIRRORS

▶ *Use mirrors properly, in good time and before signalling when . . .*

Mirrors very much come under the category of observation. The use of mirrors, apart from the two subheadings below, is dealt with in the chapter on observation.

- **On the straight:** While driving on the straight, you must check your centre mirror regularly. Every ten seconds or so should be sufficient.

- **Slowing/Stopping:** Make sure to check mirrors before braking, when slowing or when stopping. You must be aware how close behind you other vehicles are before bringing your car to a stop.

Clearance/Overtaking
Allow sufficient clearance to . . .

- **Pedestrians:** On a road where no footpath or hard shoulder exists, you must allow plenty of room for pedestrians. In this case, when you meet a pedestrian on the road, check mirrors and signal, and move out only when sure that your way ahead is clear. Remember that if your way ahead is not clear, you must yield to approaching traffic because the obstruction is on your side.

Fig. 09

- **Cyclists:** As above for pedestrians. But remember that cyclists travel in the same direction as traffic, whereas pedestrians should walk against the flow of traffic. Cyclists are vulnerable to being blown off course by gusts of wind and are also notorious for swerving to avoid potholes without notice.

- **Stationary Vehicles:** Allow at least the width of one car door between your car and stationary vehicles. Unfortunately, people often swing doors open without checking behind them. It is difficult to see pedestrians, especially children, walking out from between parked cars. Be very careful to give plenty of clearance to stationary buses, especially school buses.

- **Other Objects:** Yes! You may indicate and go out past potholes and other such obstructions provided it is safe to do so. Do not drive across foreign objects if you can avoid it. Dogs can be a nuisance; keep an eye on them and allow sufficient clearance when required.

- **Overtake Safely:** Leave plenty of room between your own car and whatever you are overtaking. Do not cut back in prematurely. Make sure you can see the vehicle in your rear-view mirror before moving back in. In the case of horses, remember that traffic can spook them easily so show some respect.

OVERTAKING
SAFELY

SIGNALS

 Give correct signals in good time.

Your tester will give you plenty of notice of the direction he wishes you to take. Use this opportunity to carry out the 'Mirror - Signal – Manoeuvre' routine in good time. Don't be afraid to ask the tester to repeat or clarify a direction for you. They will have no problem doing so. Driving instructors notice that almost 50% of people have some difficulty in distinguishing right from left when under pressure. If you think you will have any difficulty in this regard, then do some exercises to improve yourself. Even thinking about right and left during daily work can help. Believe it or not, some people even go around with a small L and R written on their hands for a day! Don't get into a panic about it, as you are certainly not the only one. Very few of us ever have to think about right and left on a normal day-to-day basis.

- **Moving Off:** Mirror - Signal - Manoeuvre. If you are pulling out to the right, signal right. If you are moving out to the left, signal left.

- **Overtaking:** If you are moving out past the white line in the centre of the road, you must indicate right. When you have passed the vehicle you are overtaking, you must indicate left to show you are moving back in again. *View* **Fig. 09** P19

- **Changing Lanes:** Indicate the direction of the lane you wish to move into. Once you have moved into that lane, cancel the signal.

- **At Roundabouts: Refer to the diagrams of the roundabout.** *View* — **Fig. 03** **Fig. 04** P14 **Fig. 05**

- **Turning Right:** Mirror, Signal right, Manoeuvre.

- **Turning Left:** Mirror, Signal left, Manoeuvre.

- **Stopping:** Your brake lights will generally be enough of a signal when slowing or stopping in traffic. If your lights are not working, use the correct hand signal shown in the diagram provided overleaf. (If your lights are not working, you will not be taken out on test.)

- **Cancel Promptly:** Leaving your indicator flashing after you have completed a manoeuvre can be confusing to others and potentially dangerous. The indicator will usually cancel itself after a turn is complete but if not, make sure you do so.

- **Hand Signals:** You must learn the hand signals and be able to perform them on request of the examiner. This used to be part of every test but it is becoming increasingly rare to be asked them. Know them all the same! *Study the diagrams opposite.*

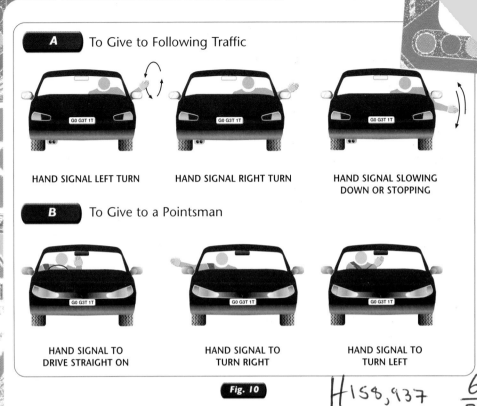

A — To Give to Following Traffic

HAND SIGNAL LEFT TURN	HAND SIGNAL RIGHT TURN	HAND SIGNAL SLOWING DOWN OR STOPPING

B — To Give to a Pointsman

HAND SIGNAL TO DRIVE STRAIGHT ON	HAND SIGNAL TO TURN RIGHT	HAND SIGNAL TO TURN LEFT

Fig. 10

● **Beckoning Others:** This is a 'grey area' where many have failed in the past. For the purpose of the test, avoid being over-courteous by beckoning (flashing, beeping or waving) anybody on to the road. If it looks as if someone is going to pull out or walk out in front of you, stop and allow them to do what they are going to do. Do not beckon them out on to the road.

● **Misleading:** Giving a misleading signal can be extremely hazardous and the tester will certainly mark it accordingly. A prime example of this is when the tester asks a driver to 'make a left turn at the second roadway to your left'. Do not indicate before the first turnoff! You may find a car will pull out of this sideroad in front of you while you are attempting to drive onto the next. Misleading signals lead to many grade 3 faults being incurred and therefore many tests being failed.

COURTESY

- **Have manners on the road!** On the day you may imagine that your driving test is the most important thing going on in the world. Do not allow this feeling to affect the common courtesy which you need to extend to other road-users. Pedestrians (being the most vulnerable users of the road) deserve particular respect. On a wet day try not to drive through large puddles which are obviously going to splash people at the roadside (the casualty list can be even higher at bus stops). No, the tester will not find this funny and you will find yourself with a grade 2 fault. The elderly, infirm and people with young children can be slow to cross a road, so show respect and wait patiently. The horn may be used to alert other road-users of your presence or the presence of any potential hazard. You may be penalised for over-use or aggressive use of the horn. Never sound your horn in close proximity to a rider on horseback. Except in emergencies, never sound your horn in a built-up area between the hours of 11:30pm and 7am. There are countless other examples of where courtesy should be shown but common sense and manners will see you through.

ALIGHTING

- When you have parked your car at the end of the test, follow this procedure. Securely apply the handbrake, put the gear lever in neutral, cancel your indicator and switch off any lights, wipers etc. which may be on. Switch off your engine and take off your seat belt. Check your outside right mirror and look over your right shoulder before opening your door. Once you and the examiner are out of your car with the doors closed, lock it.

PROGRESS

▶ *Maintain reasonable progress and avoid undue hesitancy when . . .*

Many drivers are surprised to learn that not driving the car quickly enough can be a contributing factor to failing the test. Ironically, it is the drivers who normally drive too fast who are more likely to make this mistake. Driving along the road too slowly or sitting unnecessarily long at a junction does **not** show that you are a safe driver. Driving in this manner will lead the examiner to regard you as causing an obstruction. Below is a list of the situations that appear on the examiner's sheet under the heading of progress.

● **Moving Off:** Check your mirrors, signal your intention and engage first gear. Once you have looked over your shoulder, release your handbrake and move off as soon as you see a good safe gap in the traffic. Move off briskly and get up to the speed of the flow of traffic as soon as possible. When making the decision to move off, think as if you are on your own. Do not make your decision based upon when you think the examiner would like you to go.

● **On the Straight: Driving too slowly while on the straight is a very common fault!** Drive on and move up through the gears as you would normally. If, for example, you are in an area with a speed limit of 60km/h, get your speed up towards 60km/h if the road and traffic conditions allow it. In slow-moving traffic on the straight, keep up with the flow of traffic. Make sure to leave enough distance between yourself and the car in front so you can see the two back tyres on the road beneath it. In slow traffic, if you allow the gap in front of you to grow too wide, this will encourage pedestrians to cross and cars to pull out in front of you. **Keep up with the flow.**

● **Overtaking:** Once you have moved out to overtake, accelerate a good deal after you have moved down a gear if necessary. Get the manoeuvre over and done with so you spend as little time as possible in the blind spot of the car in front and on the wrong side of the road. A word of warning! Do not cut back abruptly in front of the car you have just overtaken.

● **At Cross Junctions:** At a cross junction guarded by a stop sign, make sure to stop. As soon as you have looked each side and see that there is a safe and clear gap in the traffic, drive on.

● **At Roundabouts: The idea of the roundabout is to try to keep traffic flowing where possible.** Always begin looking to the right as you slowly approach the roundabout. At a roundabout governed by lights, make sure to obey them. When there is a safe, clear gap in the traffic coming from your right and your way ahead is clear, drive on.

● **Turning Right:** Slow down on approach but move away briskly when you see your way is clear.

- **Turning Left:** Slow down on approach but move away briskly when you see your way is clear.

- **Changing Lanes:** Move into your intended lane as soon as you have completed adequate observation, you see that your way is clear and you signal. You must adjust your speed in proportion to that of the traffic in the lane you intend to move into.

- **At Traffic Lights:** Having stopped at a red or amber light, get ready to move off again straight away. As soon as the lights turn green, check your way is clear and move off. Do not get caught having to apply the handbrake, engage first gear and find your 'point of contact' (for a detailed explanation of 'point of contact', see next chapter under clutch control) after the lights have turned green. At a set of pedestrian traffic lights, you may move off once the lights have turned flashing amber and it is safe to do so.

Your Notes:

VEHICLE CONTROLS

 Make proper use of

The Vehicle Control section involves your basic driving skills. This book will not teach you how to drive, and we recommend that you learn to drive properly with a qualified driving instructor. We have laid out below exactly what is required on your test in the use of the primary and secondary controls of the car.

● **Accelerator:** You must only ever use your right foot on the accelerator. Pressing on the accelerator increases the amount of fuel going through to your engine and therefore increases speed. A common fault is accelerating too much when coming into a junction or coming to a stop, and therefore having to stop too suddenly. When putting the clutch in to change gears, you must take your right foot off the accelerator. Failure to do this will lead your car to rev quite loudly. Not giving the car enough acceleration when moving off (especially from a hill) can lead your engine to stall. Use a controlled amount of acceleration when moving off so as not to rev too much.

● **Clutch:** Clutch control is a vital part of the test throughout all manoeuvres. Coasting is a common fault. **Travelling for any distance with the clutch fully down to the floor is known as coasting.** After a gear has been selected, you must allow the clutch back up so as to engage the new gear. When coming to a stop, make sure to brake first before clutching. Aside from coasting, you may be faulted on your lack of ability to use the clutch in a controlled manner. Being rough or too quick off the clutch leads to a bumpy drive for you and the tester. Coming too quickly off the clutch can also lead to the car cutting out.

● **Hill start:** The hill start is one of the three specific manoeuvres that you are required to complete on your test. The main aim of the hill start is to test your clutch control. The tester will ask you to stop along a kerb on a hill. Once you have stopped, put your handbrake on, put the gear lever in neutral and cancel the indicator. When you are instructed to move off, check your mirrors, paying particular attention to the outside right. Signal right. Engage first gear. Give the car some steady acceleration while at the same time bringing the clutch up a couple of inches, until you find the 'biting point' or 'point of contact'. You will know you have reached this point because of several giveaway signs. The noise of the engine will change slightly, the bonnet of your car will rise an inch or two, while the back end of the car will sit down slightly. If the engine sounds as if it is labouring at this point, then give it a little bit more acceleration. Now hold your two feet exactly as they are. Look over your right shoulder, and if your way is clear, release the handbrake and move off, looking back in the direction you are heading as you do so. Only when you have moved off and picked up some speed can you gently release the clutch the rest of the way. A common mistake at this stage is to change into second gear too early before enough speed and momentum have been built up. This leads the car to labour and even cut out. Remember you are still on a steep hill, so build up plenty of power before changing.

- **Gears:** Knowing the correct gear to select for any particular situation is a skill that is best learned through experience. You must listen to your engine as you drive. **Travelling too quickly in a low gear will cause your engine to make a 'roaring' sound. Travelling too slowly for a high gear will cause the engine to 'labour' and 'shudder'.** Driving instructors are often asked what gear the car should be in at specific places. The simple answer to that is to drive the car and change gears as and when it feels necessary and comfortable. As with all aspects of the test, don't change your driving because you think the tester would like you to. Move up and down through the gears confidently and smoothly. You are permitted to skip between fourth and second when changing down. The problem is that, if you do this without decreasing your speed using the footbrake, the transition between fourth and second will be quite rough and uncomfortable. In the interest of smooth driving, I recommend that you don't skip gears and engage each one individually. Never glide along with the car in neutral. The gear lever should only ever be in neutral when your car is stopped. Fifth gear is not usually necessary on most test routes, but do not hesitate to use it on a stretch of road where it would be appropriate.

- **Footbrake:** Smooth and effective use of the footbrake is vital. **The brake must be applied using the right foot only, never the left.** If you need to slow down for a corner, brake before it and cover the pedal as you round the corner, only applying the brake again if necessary. When bringing your car to a stop, always brake first. Only apply the clutch just before the car comes to a stop. **Practise bringing the car to a smooth stop, as if you have an imaginary cup of tea on your dashboard that you cannot spill.** Brake progressively, starting gently before gradually applying increasingly harder pressure. Try to avoid stamping suddenly on the brake except in case of emergency.

- **Handbrake:** The question of when to use the handbrake on the driving test seems to confuse many people. Its use is always required after you pull in to park. Aside from parking, the use of the handbrake is at your own discretion. If you are stopped on a hill and there is a chance that you might roll back, apply the handbrake and carry out a hill start when you mean to move off again. This applies to any time you may be stopped on a slope, either in traffic, at a junction, or during a manoeuvre such as the turnabout. Use it to avoid rolling either back or forward. Many instructors will initially encourage you to use the handbrake at a stop sign. This is to ensure that you know to stop fully but is not a requirement. The handbrake is not essential at a stop sign where the road surface is flat. Make sure to push the button in fully when applying the handbrake, thus avoiding an unpleasant crunching noise and unnecessary mechanical wear. When releasing the handbrake, make sure it is fully released before moving off. A red warning light will appear on your dashboard when your brake remains engaged.

STEERING

Examine the diagrams provided. **Fig. 11**

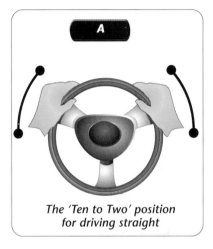

A

The 'Ten to Two' position
for driving straight

B

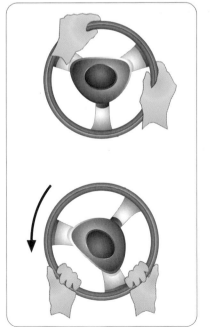

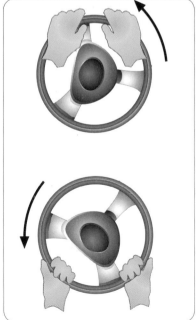

Steering Right

● **Secondary Controls:** A recently added part of the test involves the tester asking you to prove your knowledge of the secondary controls of the car. This takes place in your car at the test centre before you drive anywhere. You will need to know how to use the wipers, windscreen washer, the demister, the heated rear window, hazard warning lights, lights, horn, heater/cooler, electric windows and air conditioning where fitted. Familiarise yourself with these before your test. The position of these features varies depending on the model of your car. If you are using a car provided by a school of motoring, make sure to get your instructor to run through the car's features with you. Keep your windscreen clear throughout the test. Use wipers/washers where necessary. Make sure to switch them off when not required. If it is a dull day, put on your sidelights or dipped headlights.

● **Technical Checks:** This is another recently added part of the test. You will be asked to explain how a check would be performed on any three of the following - (a) Tyres, (b) Lights, (c) Reflectors, (d) Indicators, (e) Engine oil, (f) Coolant, (g) Windscreen washer fluid, (h) Steering, (i) Brakes, (j) Horn. Access to some of the items listed above will require you to open the bonnet and to close it securely. The location of many of these features along with the lever to open the bonnet can vary according to the make and model of vehicle you drive. It is very important to familiarise yourself with their locations before the day of the test. If you are using a car provided by an instructor, ensure that he/she runs through these features with you. Don't worry! You will not be asked to physically perform an oil change or any other mechanical task.

(a) Tyres: If the tester asks you what the minimum legal thread depth is, the answer is 1.6mm.

(b) Lights: You should know that headlights should be correctly focused and aimed. This is to ensure that the beams shine light correctly on the road ahead, do not dazzle oncoming drivers, and enable you to see properly.

(c) Reflectors: These reflect light at night in order to make other road users aware of your vehicle.

(d) Indicators: A more rapid clicking noise when you operate the indicator lever suggests that an indicator bulb has blown.

(e) Engine oil: You should be able to open the bonnet and show where the oil 'dip stick' is located and explain how it is used to determine the oil level. You should also be able to point out where oil can be added to the engine if levels are too low.

(f) Coolant: You will need to open the bonnet to show where the container for coolant is located along with the markings on this container which are used to determine levels. It is useful to know that coolant fluid generally doubles up as anti-freeze.

(g) Windscreen washer fluid: Again, this container is located under the bonnet and should be kept topped up with a mixture of water and a detergent.

(h) Steering: The power steering fluid container is also located under the bonnet. You should also know that uneven wheel balance on the car can lead to a continuous vibration in the steering wheel whilst driving.

(i) Brakes: The brake fluid container is located under the bonnet. While applying the brakes, if the pedal feels soft, spongy or slack, this often indicates that the brake fluid level is low.

(j) Horn: The car horn is usually located either on the steering wheel or on the end of the indicator lever. The horn must not be used in a build up area at night between the hours of 11.30pm and 7.00am, except in an emergency. Musical horns are not allowed on your vehicle.

Your Notes:

SPEED

▶ *Adjust speed to suit/on approach*

During your test, you must drive at an appropriate speed at all times. It goes without saying that you must stay within the legal speed limit for the area you are driving in. Speeding and speeding-related fatalities on our roads have received a huge amount of publicity lately, although the introduction of the penalty points system seems to be going some way towards raising driver awareness of this critical issue. With regard to your test, you must realise that speeding does not apply only to driving at 150 km/h. In the wrong situation you may be speeding at 10 km/h. Proper control of your speed is one of the crucial areas where you will show the examiner that you can drive with due regard for the safety and convenience of yourself and other road users. **If you do not drive safely, you will not pass!**

- **Road Conditions:** Unfortunately, many Irish roads have bad or potholed surfaces. If this is the case, then it is essential to reduce your speed and keep the drive comfortable for both yourself and the tester. Driving too fast on a bad surface can lead to lack of steering control. Cyclists and motorcyclists might steer around or be unbalanced by such road conditions. The weather can also be a huge factor in determining road conditions. You must reduce your speed to deal with adverse conditions. Heavy rain and spray reduce visibility as well as the grip your tyres have on the road. Fog and even bright sunshine can cause havoc with visibility. It is very likely that your test will be cancelled in the event of extremely wintry conditions, but take care when driving in snow or ice. Avoid steering or braking suddenly, and take extra care on corners. You must avoid skidding. Watch out for substances such as mud or oil, as these can lead the road surface to be very slippery. Warning signs may be present but pay particular attention near building sites and where agricultural work is being carried out.

- **Traffic Conditions:** All test routes involve driving through urban areas and therefore you will meet traffic. In heavy, slow-moving traffic, you will not have any choice but to move slowly. It is important, however, that you keep up with the flow of traffic. (Refer to the section on positioning for the correct distance to keep from the car in front.)

- **Roundabouts:** Slow on approach and stop if necessary. On the roundabout itself, it is important to make good progress to get around promptly, but do pay particular attention when changing lanes and exiting.

- **Cross Junctions:** Slow on approach but get away briskly.

- **Turning Right:** Slow on approach but get away briskly.

- **Turning Left:** Slow on approach but get away briskly.

- **Traffic Controls:** Pay attention and adjust your speed when encountering warning signs such as children at play, slippery surface etc. Traffic calming measures are often in place to slow you down. These measures can be in the form of road humps, chicanes or rumble strips. They are there as a warning! Apart from not impressing the tester if you do not slow down for them, they can cause damage to your car.

- **Speed Limit:** You must pay attention to signs and stay within the legal speed limit at all times.

Your Notes:

TRAFFIC CONTROLS

▶ *Comply with*

The tips below will explain very simply how you must deal with traffic controls. (You must be aware that at any traffic control where a Garda is signalling traffic, the directions of the Garda will override any lights, markings or signs present.)

● **Traffic Lights:** Red means stop. Green means go (provided it is safe). Flashing amber means you may proceed with caution provided your way ahead is clear. Solid amber means you should stop if it is safe to do so as the lights are about to turn red.

● **Traffic Signs:** You must learn them all - and, of course, obey them! Not stopping completely at a stop sign is a grade 3 fault which means you fail your test. Even if the way seems clear, stop at the white line beyond the stop sign and count three seconds to yourself before moving off. At a yield sign you may move on provided your way ahead is clear.

● **Road Markings:** Learn them and obey them! A broken white line means you may cross it but only if your way ahead is clear. A continuous white line means you must not cross except in case of emergency, or for the purpose of access. A broken line alongside a continuous line means you should obey the line nearest to you. A broken yellow line along the edge of a major road marks off where the hard shoulder begins. Junction boxes are used at tramway (LUAS) crossings in the city of Dublin. Always obey traffic lights and make sure you can cross fully without stopping on the tramway. You must keep these junction boxes fully clear at tramway crossings at all times. Never obstruct trams – remember they've no steering wheels. The regular traffic box junction is regarded as probably the most complex use of road markings.

Look over the detailed diagrams and explanation for the box junction. (Overleaf)

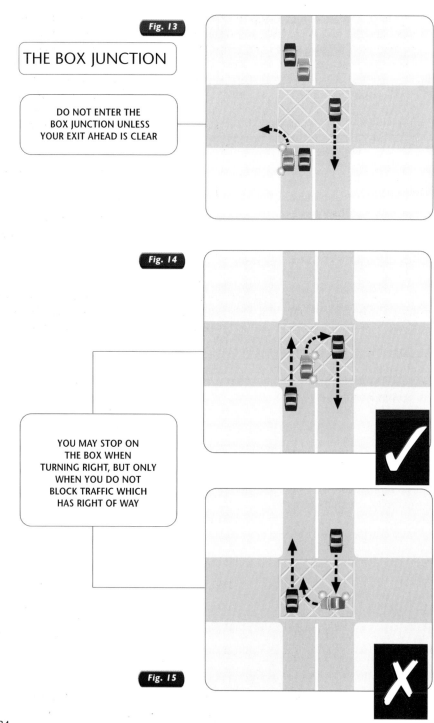

Fig. 13

THE BOX JUNCTION

DO NOT ENTER THE
BOX JUNCTION UNLESS
YOUR EXIT AHEAD IS CLEAR

Fig. 14

YOU MAY STOP ON
THE BOX WHEN
TURNING RIGHT, BUT ONLY
WHEN YOU DO NOT
BLOCK TRAFFIC WHICH
HAS RIGHT OF WAY

Fig. 15

- **Pedestrian Crossing:** Come up to pedestrian crossings expecting to have to stop. Let the tester know that you are aware of them by slowing slightly and looking both ways (even if there seems to be nobody around). Remember, flashing amber means you may proceed with caution provided that nobody is crossing or waiting to cross. You must still give way to any pedestrians. In slow-moving traffic situations, do not stop across the black and white stripes of a zebra crossing. Leave it clear until you can exit it completely on the other side. At some crossings, both sides are marked with zigzag lines. You must not overtake or park within these lines.

- **Garda/School Warden:** You must always comply fully and respectfully with their instructions.

- **Bus Lanes:** Do not drive in bus lanes during the hours in which they are in operation. It is a good idea to check these times in the area you will be doing your test in advance. They vary from place to place but most likely will be in operation during test times.

- **Cycle Lanes:** Cycle lanes are often shared with bus lanes but some are specific to bicycles. The specific type is usually highlighted with red tarmac. Keep clear of these at all times while paying attention to the fact that cyclists may swerve out without notice for a multitude of reasons.

Your Notes:

RIGHT OF WAY

▶ *Yield right of way as required.*

It is a major fault not to concede right of way when required. Read below and examine the diagrams provided.

● **Moving off:** When moving off, you must give right of way to vehicles already on the road.

● **Overtaking:** Give right of way to traffic approaching from the opposite direction. You must also give way to any vehicles already overtaking you. Do not cut in abruptly on traffic in front when moving back in.

● **Changing Lanes:** Give right of way to any traffic already in the lane you intend to move into.

● **At Junctions:** *Examine the diagrams opposite.*

● **At Roundabouts:** Give way to all traffic coming from your right and all traffic already on the roundabout.

● **Turning Right:** When turning right off a road, give way to traffic approaching from the opposite direction. For turning right at a junction, examine the diagram provided opposite.

● **Turning Left:** When turning left off a road, pay attention to cyclists travelling on your left-hand side.

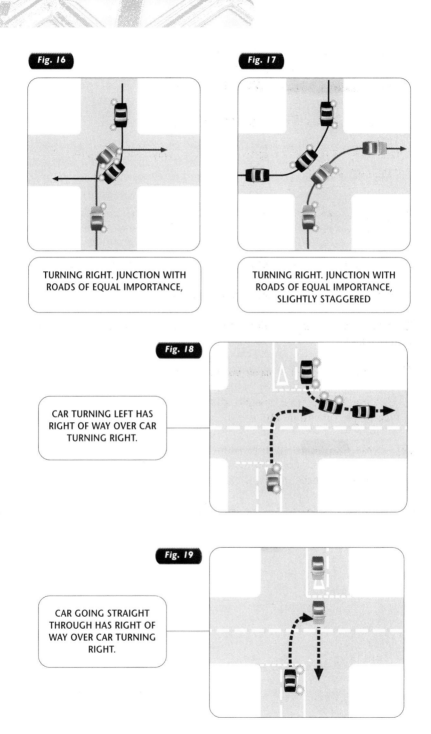

Fig. 16

TURNING RIGHT. JUNCTION WITH ROADS OF EQUAL IMPORTANCE,

Fig. 17

TURNING RIGHT. JUNCTION WITH ROADS OF EQUAL IMPORTANCE, SLIGHTLY STAGGERED

Fig. 18

CAR TURNING LEFT HAS RIGHT OF WAY OVER CAR TURNING RIGHT.

Fig. 19

CAR GOING STRAIGHT THROUGH HAS RIGHT OF WAY OVER CAR TURNING RIGHT.

REVERSING

● **Reversing**

The reverse is one of three manoeuvres that you will be required to complete. This is the part of the test which causes most apprehension and nerves. The reverse is actually quite simple and is not by any means the most common reason for failure. Most drivers rarely have to reverse from day to day, so the likelihood is that you could benefit from some practice. Do it! Reverse around as many different types of corners as possible. Do make sure it is both legal and safe to reverse around your chosen corner. (Never reverse from a minor road onto a major road.) The most common faults for the reverse are related to observation as opposed to competence (skill). Bear in mind that you do not get extra credit for completing your reverse quickly. Take your time! This will make judgment of distance much easier and you will also have a much greater chance of spotting dangers such as children. Do not risk hitting the kerb by staying too close. Leave yourself 12 to 18 inches of distance. You will need this margin for error as nerves can play a big role on the test. The tester will initially get you to pull your car in along the kerb before reaching the sideroad he intends you to reverse into. He will then explain what he wants you to do. He will get you to pull out, drive past the junction and pull in again approximately two car lengths from the corner on the other side.

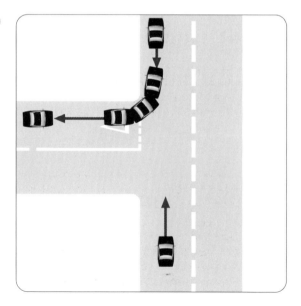

Fig. 20

● Competently

As you pull in before the reverse, make sure you are parallel to the kerb and have your steering wheel straight. Stay 12 to 18 inches out from the kerb. When you move off, keep your two hands on the wheel. Control the speed of the car by manipulating the clutch at the biting point. This slow speed control will give you time to make decisions. Do not begin to steer until you have reached the beginning of the corner. Looking over your left shoulder, when you see the beginning of the corner come into your rear side window, begin to steer. Do not over-steer. Once you put on an estimated lock, hold it to see what it is doing for you as you move. If you then see that your lock is too much or too little, adjust slightly. Do not constantly adjust and readjust. Once you have got around to the point where the kerb straightens out and your car is parallel to the kerb, begin to straighten your wheel. Only bring your steering wheel back to the point where it is straight (the logo in the centre of the steering wheel should be upright). If you take the wheel back any further than this, the rear of your car will start to come out into the road. When you have reached this point with your car and steering wheel straight, you should be parallel to the kerb. Keep reversing until the examiner tells you to stop. The position of your car on completion should be the same in relation to the kerb as it was at the beginning. Put your handbrake on and put the gear lever into neutral.

● Observation

Look into the roadway you are about to reverse into as you pass it before pulling in. Look all around before moving off, making note of any children, bikes, traffic or other potential hazards. On moving off, you should be looking over your left shoulder. Your outside left mirror should be used only as a guide and requires only the briefest of glances. Before you begin to steer into the corner, have a full look around to the front and look back again. On the corner itself, once the front of the car begins to swing out into the road, look around to your right. Again look back. Continue to look back in the direction you are travelling until you bring the car to a stop. Mirrors contain many blind spots and their use on the reverse should be kept to a minimum where a good view can be obtained out of the rear and rear-side windows.

● Right of way

Give right of way to any vehicle coming out of the road you are reversing into. You may see a vehicle coming out of the road as you pass to pull in at the start. This vehicle must be allowed to exit the junction before you proceed. On moving off, when you look around to your right and see a vehicle approaching, allow them to pass before swinging your front end out. If a vehicle approaches you from behind as you are reversing, **stop**. Usually they will see your reverse lights and move to go around you. If, however, they sit behind you, then move carefully forward around the corner to your original position.

TURNABOUT

▶ The Turnabout

The turnabout is sometimes referred to as a "three-point turn". However, the manoeuvre does not have to be completed in three moves. The roadways chosen are often too narrow to allow this. Many of the test routes have a turnabout in a residential area. This means that a lot of attention must be paid to the dangers of children, bikes, dogs etc. As with the reverse, the most common faults on this manoeuvre are related to observation as opposed to skill (competence). Proper observation before moving off will help to avoid the extra pressure of having a vehicle waiting to pass as you turn in the road. Practice will greatly improve your chances of completing a nice tidy turnabout on your test. Cars come in many shapes and sizes so it is important to familiarise yourself with the exact length and width of your own vehicle.

This is something that you have to do for yourself by practising.

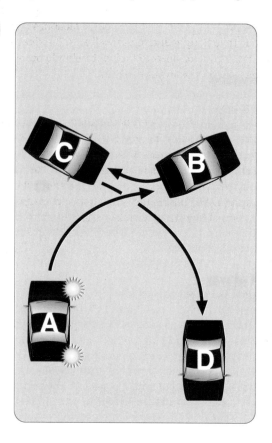

Fig. 21

● Competently

Turn the steering wheel, passing the wheel through your hands (do not cross your hands over) *Examine Figs. 11 & 12*. Only steer while the car is moving. Control your speed with your clutch (only bring your clutch up to the point where your car begins to move). The more slowly you move, the more time you have to steer. The more you can steer, the fewer moves it will take to get the car around. Turning the car in three moves shows impressive vehicle control and is ideal. To bump into a kerb is a grade 2 fault, while to mount a kerb is a grade 3 fault thus meaning failure. Do not risk trying to get the car around in three moves if there is a chance that you will hit the kerb. To do it in 5 or even 7 moves is fine. Apply your handbrake after each move if there is a slope on the road. This will prevent you from rolling forwards or backwards into the kerb.

● Observation

Before moving off look around in all directions. Turn your head to look over both shoulders and take note of any cars, pedestrians, cyclists etc. In a residential area, do not move off if you notice a car coming out of a driveway close to you, as it will probably be coming in your direction. While you are moving off, continue to look right and left as well as in the direction you are travelling. While reversing, turn your head to look out behind you over your shoulders. It is not enough only to look in your mirrors.

● Right of Way

This is very much tied-in with observation. There is no point in looking all around if you do not react to what you see. Allow all traffic to pass before you move off. You may have to allow vehicles to pass while you are completing the manoeuvre. Generally, other traffic will wait and allow you to finish. Carry out the manoeuvre promptly and without undue hesitancy. Getting it over and done with is the best way to avoid causing too much of an obstruction. If children or cyclists come close to you at any stage, stop and allow them to pass.

Parking

Parking may refer to when you pull in at the side of the road before or after a manoeuvre. When you return to the test centre after the test, you will be expected to park within a reasonable distance from the centre. Make this as simple as possible for yourself. If you can drive straight into a space then do so. At some test centres it may be necessary to reverse or parallel park into a space. Practise this yourself.

- ## Competently
  Control your speed when coming in to park. If you are parking beside a kerb, make sure that you do not bump into it. Do not finish up more than 12 to 18 inches from it. Once you have finished, follow the routine of Handbrake, Neutral, Cancel the indicator.

- ## Observation
  Check your rear-view mirror and your outside left mirror before indicating left if pulling in on that side. If reversing into a space, check all three of your mirrors as well as looking over both shoulders before you begin to reverse. While reversing, look over your shoulder again on the side that your front wing is about to swing out. When exiting your car, always check your mirror and look around before you open your door.

- ## Legally
  Do not park on double yellow lines at any time. Always make sure that all four of your tyres are inside any white lines that may mark out a parking space.

The Evening Before your Test

The Evening Before your Test

You should prepare everything you need in advance of the day of the test. The idea is to have as little stress and running around as possible on the day. It never fails to amaze me how many people discover within hours of the test that their licence is out of date or their brake lights are not working. Worse still is when they do not discover until the examiner refuses to take them out because of it! **Take a look at the check list below and tick off each point as you ensure it is taken care of.** If you have any doubts about whether your car is roadworthy or the discs are all in date, arrange to hire a car from your driving school. They will make sure that everything is in order in this respect and save you a lot of hassle.

On a personal level, you should try to relax as much as possible. Go for a drive or, better still, have a driving lesson. Have a quick recap over the road signs and rules of the road questions but don't study late into the night. Finish up early and go for a walk, watch some TV or do whatever else relaxes you. Going to the pub for some early 'Dutch courage' might seem like a good idea at the time but the trauma of a driving test with a hangover is definitely not advisable!

CHECK LIST:

● Make sure that your provisional licence will be current on the date of your test. If your test date is after the expiry date of your licence, the motor tax office will issue you with a new one to cover you for that date. The licence must also be relevant for the category of vehicle in which you wish to take the test. (The car is category B).

● You must be insured to drive the vehicle you are providing for the test. The vehicle must clearly display a current valid insurance disc, which must clearly show the registration number of the vehicle and the policy dates. (A driving school will have taken care of this if you are hiring a car from them.)

● Current valid motor tax disc.

- Any car obliged to have one must display a current valid NCT disc.

- Proper 'L' plates must be fitted to the front and rear of your vehicle.

- Clear your windscreen of all unnecessary visual obstructions. Give the car a bit of a clean-out so there are no empty containers or tools rattling around. Clean the windows, mirrors and number plates.

- Have somebody stand outside your car and check that your brake and indicator lights are working. You will not be taken out if even one is broken.

- Make sure there are no system warning lights on your dashboard. If there are, get the problem sorted by a mechanic as soon as possible. Have enough fuel and oil in your car. You don't want 'low fuel' warning lights coming on before or during the test.

- Mechanically, your car must comply with the following. The tyres must have a minimum thread depth of 1.6mm. The seat belts, doors and head restraints must be present and in full working order.

- The suspension should not be obviously defective. The exhaust should be functional. The handbrake should be in good working order.

- **Check your letter from the department to make sure you know the exact time and location of your test!** If you are not there on time, the test will not be conducted and you will forfeit your fee.

The Day of Your Test

▶ *The Day of Your Test:*

Have a last run-through your check-list and make sure you have your provisional licence with you.

Most people find that a last pre-test lesson before the test is very beneficial. This last lesson will help you to get rid of any last-minute nerves and get you used to the traffic and road conditions on that particular day. If it's not possible to have a lesson, then go for a drive around the test route yourself. Even if you are familiar with the routes, there may be new roadworks or it may be rubbish collection or beer delivery day.

Get yourself to the test centre at least 15 minutes early. Find a good parking space that you can drive out of easily. If there is a carpark, reverse into a space so that when you come out with the tester, you will be able to drive straight out of the space. (Remember that when you come back from the test, you can drive straight into a space unless the tester requests differently.) Get inside the test centre and be seated in the waiting area with at least ten minutes to spare. The tester may like to take you out early and get finished early which naturally will make him happy!

Last-minute run-through of things to think about on the actual test:

- *Listen carefully to the directions given to you by the tester.* If you are in any doubt, ask him to clarify his instructions.

- *You will need excellent all-round observation.* Don't be afraid to move your head. Look into sideroads as you pass.

- *Drive neatly and precisely with accurate road positioning.* Remember the correct positions for turning right, left and going straight on.

- *Control your car like you are in charge.* Control your speed rounding corners and on all manoeuvres. Use your gears well and change down in time before making a turn off.

- *Keep up with the flow of traffic.* Make normal progress and avoid causing an obstruction. Don't be afraid to change up through the gears as required. Don't sit in junctions for any longer than is necessary.

- *Be alert and have good hazard awareness.* Plan ahead and try to take note of anything which will potentially come into your path or affect your driving.

- *Be confident and think positive.* Even if you do make a mistake it does not mean you have failed. Stay calm and continue on as normal. Remember, you can make a number of minor errors and still pass. If the car cuts out, turn the key again and get on with it. Don't sit there beating yourself up and causing an obstruction. *Good Luck!*

Your Notes:

Your Notes:

Your Notes:

Your Notes: